Praise for
The Truth in

"What I love most about ~~the book is that it was~~ written with integrity, passion and knowledge, which in my opinion, demonstrates 'TRUTH!' The author has taken his experiences and success in Network Marketing and written a no-nonsense, inspiring, and easy-to-read book that will benefit all individuals who hope to rise to the top in this arena."

Marilyn Rose
Certified Professional Coach
ELI-MP, PCC

"Phil Benson has been a professional associate and friend of mine for over twenty years. I have been in the network marketing industry for over fifty years full-time and have learned a lot from Phil. He has a way of explaining something as complicated and misunderstood as network marketing and presenting it in such a way that "newbies" and seasoned leaders can benefit from. This book is much needed in the industry and should be in the hands of every network marketer, new and old. Phil has done an excellent job in bringing to light the lies and truths about an industry I love and worked in for over fifty years."

—Dave Stoltzfus
Master distributor

"Phil Benson is a one of a kind trainer with a keen eye to discern what works and what doesn't. If you dream of a successful future in network marketing, don't miss this surefire book for success."

Nancy Thompson,
Diamond Distributor

THE **TRUTH** IN **NETWORK MARKETING**

CROSSING THE BRIDGE ON YOUR JOURNEY TO SUCCESS

Phil Benson

MEDIA

Published 2019 by Gildan Media LLC
aka G&D Media
www.GandDmedia.com

Energetic Self Perception Chart on page 91 © Bruce D. Schneider
1999, 2006, 2018

Front cover design by David Rheinhardt of Pyrographx

Interior design by Meghan Day Healey of Story Horse, LLC

Library of Congress Cataloging-in-Publication Data is available
upon request

ISBN: 978-1-7225-0296-6

10   9   8   7   6   5   4   3   2   1

I want to dedicate this book to two people.
The first is my dad, Lou.
Not often is a father a son's best friend,
the best man at his wedding, a business partner,
and his greatest supporter. My dad was all
of the above. I will never forget him.

The second is my wife, Rene.
It is rare that a wife is always there,
supporting her husband in all he does in all
aspects of his life. Rene has been there
supporting me in every business venture,
every marathon I've run, and every decision
I've had to make. Thank you, Rene.

CONTENTS

FOREWORD

by Ed Wiens

first met Phil Benson over twenty years ago, when we were both working our way up the ladder in network marketing. Though we were in different branches of the company, I quickly developed an appreciation for the responsible, professional, and ethical manner in which Phil conducted his business and personal relationships—the glue that holds this profession together.

Phil's work here is a masterful depiction of what network marketing truly is and, equally importantly, what it is not—or shouldn't be. His perspective is wise counsel for the newcomer to the industry as

well as for the seasoned veteran. It is especially valuable for those considering joining the profession for
the first time—at whatever level of ambition. If you've
dismissed the validity of network marketing for any
number of reasons, you owe it to yourself to see what
Phil has to say.

Having been involved as a career network-
marketing professional for over three decades (from
the pay phone, fax machine, and cassette-tape era
to the web-connected world of today), I've seen
the good, bad and the ugly of the industry, as has
Phil. Follow his advice, and you can fast-track your
learning curve to make your way through the jungle
of hype and misinformation and put your business
building efforts on a solid, well-marked path to the
mountaintop.

If you learn from Phil, I'm confident that, like
me, you'll conclude that there is no more noble, fair,
honest, and rewarding way to earn a living than in
building a solid network-marketing business. Nothing
compares. As Eric Worre says, "Network marketing
isn't perfect, just better." It will provide you with an
equal opportunity to become as *unequal* as you want
to be, and it will afford you an opportunity to make a
difference while making a living.

Finally, if you apply Phil's instructions here, you'll simply be a better you, regardless of how high you climb up the ladder of success in network marketing.

Ed Wiens is a network-marketing professional, industry speaker and trainer, multimillion-dollar earner, and leader of a global team of tens of thousands.

PREFACE

~⌘~

by Phil Benson

Being a serial entrepreneur, I have been involved in all types of businesses. I have worked on the floor of the American Stock Exchange, built two mobile-home communities, had an insurance agency, had a home-improvement business, become a certified life coach and many more—too numerous to mention here.

When I was introduced to network marketing, a fire in my belly appeared that I had never before experienced in my business life. Here was a business that gave me everything an entrepreneur could wish for. A business that could be worked anywhere you lived, with no employees, no overhead, no inventory.

A business that was a win-win for all involved, if they took the time to learn and understand the business model. I dove into the business and worked hard and, at times, long hours. But I loved it. The people I met and worked with and the friendships that developed were worth the effort.

As I began to think about retirement or what I could do to keep busy in my seventies, I knew I had to share what I knew about network marketing. I wanted to help future network marketers as well as those now working their networking business.

The book you are about to read was written with one purpose in mind: How can I help people find success in network marketing and reach their goals? Network marketing has given me so much in my life that I felt I had to give back to the people who were on their journey to find success.

In network marketing, it is all about the journey. One keeps striving to be a better person and in turn to help other people grow on their journeys. My wish for all is to enjoy the journey and always strive to be the best you can be.

INTRODUCTION

❦

In the Beginning

Twenty-seven years ago, I sold a real-estate development, which allowed me to buy a new home and relieved me of the financial burden most people feel at midlife. Once the sale was complete and I no longer had an office to go to, I searched for something to do. I was your typical type A personality. I was an athlete, and usually by 9 a.m. I had run ten miles, biked twenty-five miles, or swum.

But what could I do now when the day started? That was my quandary. I'd never worked for anyone, as I was a serial entrepreneur, having started several businesses. Many were failures, although a few generated successes. The sale of the development was a home run. But I was still young, in my fifties, and needed something to stimulate me and, more important, a goal to strive for.

One phone call changed my life. It was from my father, who was retired and living in Florida. My dad was my best friend, my best man at my wedding, and on and off a business partner. Like me, he was a serial entrepreneur. I sat down with him recently, and went over how many businesses he'd started or was involved in before he retired. Can you believe thirty-seven? As in my case, some were failures and some successes.

Always looking for opportunities, even in retirement, my father had been walking around a flea market with a friend when he came upon a table with unique products he'd never seen before. There was a business opportunity there. Obviously he was talking to a good salesman that day, but my dad was thinking this might be an opportunity for his son.

The next day I got the phone call. My dad said he'd seen products that were life-changing and heard stories of people who'd been helped physically. And, he said, you can make lots of money selling these. He told me I could buy the products to try them myself. He asked for my credit card—and who was I to refuse my dad? He told me he'd send me some products, and if they weren't any good, the "salesman" said my dad could return them.

Three days later the doorbell rang, and there was the UPS man holding five boxes, two of which were huge. I opened them and indeed saw products I had never seen or heard of. But the big shock came when I saw the receipt. Twenty-five hundred dollars had been charged to my credit card. I called my dad, told him the products had arrived, and asked if he knew how much they'd cost. He simply said, "Don't worry; you can return them if you don't want them." He gave me the name and number of the "salesman" and told me to call him so he could explain the business to me.

That was my introduction to network marketing (NM). I was one of few people my age who'd never been approached or invited to attend an NM seminar. This was during the growth of Amway and several other NM giants. I never knew why no one ever called to invite me to an opportunity meeting. Well, I owed it to my dad to at least investigate this business opportunity. I called the salesman and found out this indeed was NM, and he was an independent distributor for his company. I told him I had no clue what NM was and asked if he could come up from Florida to tell me about the business and show me how the products worked (this was before all the technical advances that have changed how NM is done). He said he could not, because the trip was too expensive, but, he'd mail me videos and cassettes that could explain the products and the business opportunity. My upline (as NM terminology has it) was not a salesman but an independent distributor.

My journey in NM began. Several days later, tapes and cassettes arrived and I immersed myself in learning all I could. I learned that if indeed these products did what my dad and upline said they did, there could be a chance to make money. I watched the tapes over and over again. Since there were no meetings to go to in my area, I decided to conduct a meeting at home and duplicate what I saw on the videos. The videos said to invite family and friends and make the presentation exactly as they demonstrated. So that's what I did.

I was lucky in that twelve people showed up. No one bought anything, and no one signed up. But I will never forget what a good friend said to me: "Phil, this is not for me, but I know you will be very successful. I have never seen you so excited." I proceeded to give ten presentations before I went to one that was a two-hour drive away. The rest, as they say, is history.

My twenty-five-year journey in NM has taken me to the top ranks of two NM companies, and I've had experiences with several others. I helped the companies open in eight countries as I built an international business. First and foremost, I discovered that NM is the best and fairest business model today. It is available to all people, no matter their race, sex, or financial situation. It rewards those who apply themselves to the principles taught for success. But there are some caveats of which one must be aware.

Born in the 1940s, network marketing has overcome early challenges and found huge success, but there has always been a misconception about how it works and whether one can indeed attain all that is promised from the opportunity. New prospects and distributors are sometimes fooled by what they hear, and they can't make an informed decision. But even those already involved in NM can benefit from reevaluating their approach in building their team. This book is for all of those people.

The bottom line: when a person grows their business with integrity, leads with the truth, and understands that NM is never about oneself, everyone benefits.

I am not here to teach you how to be successful in network marketing. But I can guide you in building a successful NM team by being honest and truthful about what this exciting and dynamic business model can be.

Network marketing can be divided into several areas. The first has to do with understanding the business model and grasping the tools necessary to implement it. In these pages, you will find my approach to the business model, a list of books that teach you how to be a good networker and explain what must be learned to succeed, and an outline of what I consider the heart of NM: *personal growth.* I will show you how to gauge where you are as an individual and help you examine your ability to communicate and interact with others. Understand that NM is never about sales—it is about building and leading a team of people. To be able to do that, one must understand oneself better. One must also be comfortable in dealing with other people in all situations.

CHAPTER ONE

~

The Truth Behind
the Lies

I am a strong believer in network marketing. As I said, I have been associated with the industry for over twenty-five years, both as a user of products and a builder of teams. But I'm bothered by the tendency to exaggerate and even lie to entice people to try NM.

There is no need to resort to untruths. This industry has been around for well over sixty years and has grown into one that provides many people with a vehicle to a secure future. But many have turned away from it because they perceive it to be run by people out for their own success alone, who are doing and saying anything to get others involved.

These lies are not told by everyone in the industry, but those who do tell them overshadow and hurt the integrity of those building their business the right way. When people are led down the wrong path and leave the industry, they often generalize that everyone is wronged the way they were. This perception must be changed. The only way to do that is for all participants in the business model to be truthful.

Below is a look at several of the lies told to new and prospective distributors as well as the corresponding truths and what could be said to present a positive and truthful picture to a person interested or beginning in NM.

Lie 1.

"If I can do it, you can do it," "If John can do it, you can do it," or "If Mary can do it, you can do it."

The Truth

A prospect looking at a network-marketing opportunity will hear these statements more times than any other. Why? Because NM is all about promoting the dream and teasing people into believing that if someone else did it, you can too. I am not saying that the person cannot do it, but the real question that should be asked when someone says, "If I can do it, you can do it," is, "So tell me what it took for you do it. How long did it take; how much support did you have? Were you new to NM when you started, or did you have experience?"

A great deal goes into why someone made it in NM. It is unfair and misleading to compare one person's success to another's. It's like saying that John made it to the major leagues in baseball, so you can also. Sure, the opportunity is there, but do you have the skills to carry you to the big leagues? Is the desire the same and the work ethic the same?

There is a story about two men who opened barbershops across the street from each other. When they opened, both had the opportunity to be successful. But one became a success while the other closed. Why would that happen? Both were in the same town, started at the same time, and had success as their goal. Obviously the man who survived had the necessary tools to be successful. He was personable, skilled in cutting hair, and able to manage his business professionally, and he understood his market and had the drive to do what it took. The other did not.

When speaking to a prospect, is it fair to say, "If John can do it, you can do it," without telling the prospect what John did to succeed? Was he an experienced network marketer? Did he already have the skills needed to build a successful team? Did he understand what leadership knowledge he'd need? These are just a few of the skills and experience one needs to be successful.

The Lie Corrected

Here is a conversation that would better serve the prospect. Network marketer Bob to prospect Bill: "Bill, see John over there? He has become successful in NM, just as you can. But he worked hard, he learned the skills, he committed to reach his goals, and basically he did whatever it took to become successful. Bill, if you commit to do what it takes to be successful as John did, and if you keep at it, the opportunity is there for you."

One of the biggest mistakes a network marketer can make is to paint false hopes and dreams. Be honest, be truthful, and build your business with integrity. Lying to someone will only make it harder for that person to succeed. Their belief system will be compromised. and overcoming their false assumptions will be more difficult.

Lie 2.

"This is a ground-floor opportunity; it is the best time to get involved."

The Truth

I have been involved with two companies seriously and have taken a look at several others. At every introductory meeting I've gone to, someone has always said, "This is a ground-floor opportunity; it is the best time to get involved." Why would one company say this when it had been started ten years earlier, and why would another say it after it had been a going business fifteen years? I did hear the statement at two newly established companies, which could argue that they were indeed ground-floor opportunities. But that is debatable also.

What exactly is a ground-floor opportunity? There are several ways to analyze that claim. It could mean the company is brand-new and is just starting to build its base of leaders, so now would be the perfect time to get involved. It could also mean that the company is offering a breakthrough product; thus this is a ground-floor opportunity to promote it. Another scenario would be that the company has been around a while but has not established its field leadership, so now could be a ground-floor opportunity to get involved with growing the leadership.

The Lie Corrected

Ground-floor opportunity is a catchphrase that's been used in the network-marketing industry since the beginning. It is the core of bringing the dream of success to its prospects. When you hear the phrase, you immediately believe that this company is offering you the perfect chance to hit a home run. The problem is that *ground-floor opportunity* rarely means an opportunity that's truly special, that no one else has heard about.

When I started hearing the phrase, I began looking into each company that used it to see if indeed there was a special opportunity with unique timing or unique products. In most cases, it was just a phrase used to hype the opportunity.

In my eyes, for a company to be a true ground-floor opportunity, several things have to be in place. First, the company's corporate leaders have to have network-marketing experience. Second, the product has to be unique and tested and has to appeal to the whole population. Third, the company has to be able to expand globally in a few years. Finally, the company has to have been in business at least three years and is beginning to have a track record of growth.

Each year many new companies a year enter the NM arena. I can guarantee you that 99 percent will use the phrase "ground-floor opportunity." Why? Because they want to entice prospects with the chance to be the first to join. Here is a hard fact: over 90 percent of first-time companies will fail by their second year, if not their first. The odds of being the first in a new company are slim. Most companies have master distributors, who bring their leaders, who bring their teams to the company. Thus the average prospect will not experience a true ground-floor opportunity. That does not mean they won't succeed. More about that later.

How do we correct the language and meaning of "this is a ground-floor opportunity, and this is the best time to get involved"? Do away with the promotional language completely. Replace it with fact. Change the language, and be honest with the prospect. Why not say, "The opportunity with our company is special. Yes, it is a new company, but we are just beginning to grow, and we are looking for people who want to work hard and take advantage of this new opportunity"? Or, if the pitch is for the product,

Lie 4.

"If you are a salesman, you will be successful."

The Truth

Most people are introduced to NM through the product a company is selling. If you have a sales background or love to promote products, and the person who has introduced you to the product knows that, these are the next words you will hear: "Since you are a salesman, you will be very successful at this."

That is far from guaranteed. NM is not a sales business in the true sense. Selling a product is one aspect of the business, but only a small one. Let's take a minute to understand how important selling actually is to your success.

It is a fact that products must be sold for a NM company to be successful. But being able to sell products does not mean the distributor will be successful. A distributor could have the ability to sell many products but lack the other skills needed to build the business, which will leave him far short of achieving the top levels of the company. The successful network marketer must have many other skills to be successful. Among them are leadership, team building, ability to motivate, goal setting, and planning. Sales skills form a very small part of success in NM.

The Lie Corrected

When promoting the business to a prospect who has one of the skills needed in NM, the distributor can get excited and exploit that as bait. Again, however you must be honest. Yes, if he loves to sell and is good at it, tell him so, but explain that while this is part of the business, it is only a small part of being a successful distributor. If he agrees to sign up believing that he will be successful because he's a salesman, you have failed him. You must explain that if the only skill he utilizes is selling, he'll be able to earn *some* money, but not the big money he's heard about. Also, he won't experience duplication, the heart of NM.

Lie 5.

"You don't have to sell products; you just have to recruit people."

The Truth

This statement is a double-edged sword. First, you do have to sell products, and second, just recruiting people will not guarantee your success.

Let's look at the first part: "You don't have to sell products." Most NM companies require you to sell a minimum number of products, and they give you incentives to sell. Thus selling *is* a part of the business. But in NM, selling is not traditional selling. I like to call it "sharing." You share by telling a story of what the product has done for you. You can also share by giving the customer a sample and letting her experience it in the hope that she becomes a repeat customer. NM is not a high-pressure sale. It is just the opposite.

Now let's look at the second part: "You just have to recruit people." I have seen distributors recruit many people personally, yet never progress past the lower ranks. Why? NM is *not* just about recruiting people.

You hear the saying throughout the industry: "Throw a lot of people on the wall, and some will stick." But the new distributor who has successfully recruited a surge of many new distributors will quickly become discouraged if none of those recruits can duplicate her in recruiting; thus she will see little success moving forward in the company. In my first company, I only recruited about twenty-five people over several years, yet three of them led me to becoming a millionaire earner. It was definitely not my recruiting prowess, because I know distributors who have recruited hundreds of people without the same success. It was because I'd learned all the other skills necessary to be successful.

Most people do not like to sell, so the distributor tells them it is not necessary and that all they'll have to do is recruit. That might get them started, but then what if they also don't have the skills to recruit and lead? Where does that leave them? Simply struggling to succeed.

The Lie Corrected

In network marketing, products must be sold. Why tell someone they don't have to sell products? Explain that it's not the traditional method of selling. Many companies give you free samples or discounts on products so you can give them to prospects to try. In essence, you are letting the product do the selling. You are also using your own experience with the product.

To avoid the lie, simply state that the traditional method of selling is not used—that instead we share the product and its stories. Add that recruitment skills are necessary, but not the only skills needed to get to the top. Be honest.

Lie 6.

"With a little work, you can earn a lot of money."

The Truth

How many times have we heard that one? It could be the single most common sentence for getting someone's attention and motivating them. But I have been in the business world for over forty years and haven't yet met someone who can say, "This happened to me." Oh, yes, it has happened to people who have money, invest in a business, and after time get a big payoff—they did no more than invest! But 99 percent of people don't have that kind of money, nor do they have the right person or opportunity to invest in.

A lot of people portray network marketing as a business in which all you have to do is present an opportunity to people and you will be on your way to getting rich. This is as far from the truth as you can get. This lie has two parts.

First: "With a little work." To be successful in network marketing—and I mean to reach the top ranks and make a lot of money—you have to put in the hours and *work* the business hard. Don't let anyone tell you differently. When I first started out in my initial company, I had no preconceptions. I only knew that if you want to be successful in a business, you have to put in the time and work, so that is what I did. It took me five years and a lot of long hours to reach the top levels. One year I spent eight months traveling the world, building my international business. It was interesting to see the world, but it was a lot of work and time away from my family. With the second company in which I was successful, I reached the top in a shorter period, but not with any less work. I just had more experience to guide me along.

When you hear the words "with a little work," stop and ask the person what he means by that. Ask him to give you the background behind what he has accomplished and the money he is making. Network marketing requires time, commitment, persistence, and hard work if you want to be truly successful.

Now for the second part: "You can earn a lot of money." "A lot of money" means different things to different people. Let's clarify. Five hundred dollars a month could be a mortgage payment, a car payment, or a payment toward a credit card. To many, that is a lot of money. Others may think that $1,000 to $2,000 per month would let them enhance their lifestyle—to them, that is a lot of money. After that, $5,000 to $10,000 per month might mean someone could quit their job and do this business full-time—yet again, a lot of money. Finally, those making $25,000 to $100,000 and above per month in NM can honestly say they *are* making a lot of money. It is important that you have a definition of what "a lot of money" means to you.

To be honest, when you are at a business presentation and hear the presenter talk about making a lot of money, he is painting the dream for everyone and wants you to think about the last amount I mentioned. He is there to get you excited and in so doing probably does not have your best interests at heart.

The Lie Corrected

Let's put the sentence together: "With a little work, you can earn a lot of money." If a lot of money to you is $250 to $500 per month, you'll have to put in some work part-time. Not a lot, but you have to commit to a schedule to do the business every day to generate the income It could be one to three hours done consistently each and every day. Understand that in all NM companies, the average income is in the neighborhood of $250 per month.

To get to the next level, you are going to have to put in more time and effort, consistently and persistently. Here you will begin to experience what is really needed to get to the higher levels. If that's what you want, a true commitment is going to have to be made. You probably can't afford to go full-time, so you will have to put in hours that are equivalent to having a second job. Here you will truly understand how big a lie the initial statement was.

The real misconception is that when you hear about people making $25,000 and more, you think they are now on easy street and spending their time doing whatever they want. How wrong that belief is! The ones making the big money in NM are the hardest workers. When I was making over $40,000 per month, I'd never worked harder. I am friendly with a lady who makes well over $200,000 per month. She is on the road most of the year, traveling all over the world, giving presentations and speeches to small and large groups. She has to love it, but it is *work*.

What do you say to avoid the lie? When talking to people, first ask them what would they be satisfied with making after six months. Listen to them and then answer realistically what they'd have to do to accomplish that. Tell them the amount of time they'd need to spend working, the number of people they'd need to talk to, and the tools they'd need to reach their goals. As the amount they'd like to earn goes up, again be honest with them and tell them it will involve work done consistently and that they must be totally focused on their goal.

Network marketing is a real business model, one I believe to be the fairest model in business for all involved. Yet as with any business, to be successful and earn considerable money, you must *work* at it. It is not easy, but you can begin the journey immediately with the proper guidance. That is the beauty of network marketing. My mentor told me it would take five years to truly understand network marketing. After five and a half years, I looked at my wife and said, "I got it."

Lie 7.

"Anyone can do this business."

The Truth

You can say that anyone can pursue this business in a general sense, but not everyone can be successful at it. Since the entry-level monetary investment in most NM companies is relatively small ($100 to $1,000+), almost anyone *can* start in the business. Thus people use the statement "anyone can do this business" as a hook to get others involved.

But the real lie is "everyone can do the business." I can play golf, but can I be a successful professional golfer? No, because there are skills that have to be learned, time that has to be allocated, money that has to be spent beyond my initial investment, and, most of all, a commitment to a goal that has to be made. When a new prospect hears the statement, "Anyone can do this business," they're being misled about what it entails.

In the beginning of my journey, I tried signing anyone up to my team who would listen to me. I believed that if they would speak to enough people and follow the system, they would succeed. What I found out was a lot different. There are books and tools that can help one master the basics—if a commitment to mastering the basics is there. (See chapter 2.) But the most underrated and misunderstood component of network marketing is personal growth—which requires work on a deeper level.

Most people, when they start a job or even a business, do not expect it to change their personal makeup. Network marketing is a business where you are interacting with people on a nearly constant basis. You must be prepared to understand their needs and wants. In order to do that well, you must be able to understand your own blocks, limitations, and assumptions. It's going to take time and work on yourself to grow to a point where you can confront your personal challenges. To be able to see inside yourself will take a lot of personal-growth books, seminars, and confronting what might be holding you back in life. This is not an overnight learning process; it can take several years to grasp NM. You can grow a business during that time, but a lot of work watching others do it and reading and growing must take place if you want to one day be called a professional networker. Chapter 3 of this book will help you with this.

The Lie Corrected

So what should be said instead of "anyone can do this business"? The only purpose served by that statement is to get a prospect involved. If prospects had a better understanding of what it took to become a success and knew the road they'd have to travel, they wouldn't so quickly blame the network marketer who got them into it.

When talking to a new prospect, one might say, "Network marketing can be done by most people, but it has some caveats. First, it is a business that require skills that must be learned. Several challenges in the business must be mastered. These include handling objections, presenting your business plan, showing leadership, public speaking, training people, personal growth, and many others. If you are willing to commit the time needed to learn and implement those skills, then my team and I can help you on your journey."

Just remember that even all the honesty and offering of help in the world cannot guarantee someone's success. You see, network marketing *isn't* for everyone. Many begin the journey but can't master the skills. They lose motivation, let life get in the way, or just give up when they don't find success quickly enough. When that happens, even after you've given your time and help, you need not feel bad—it was they who gave up.

Lie 8.

"You can build this business with as little as a $100 investment."

The Truth

When was the last time someone approached you and said, "I know of a business that can make you a huge amount of money, and you can start it with a $100 investment"? Probably never, unless it was a network-marketing distributor who was pulling all the strings they could to get you involved.

The enticement of making a lot of money with little investment is too good for most people to disregard. Hearing the statement, the prospect wants to hear more, and then the unscrupulous distributor throws some more enticements his way. He will continue to do this until the prospect takes the bait and joins the team.

It *is* possible for a prospect to start in a new company where one or two of the first people he speaks to are superstars, and these people *could* propel him to higher ranks, where he *would* have the ability to earn good money. But the odds are slim that this will happen sooner rather than later.

Along the way, this is what is more likely to happen. Most companies require a monthly product minimum that ranges from $50 to $150. Then there are meetings to attend, which entail more expenses—these range from $10 for local meetings to a couple hundred dollars for regional meetings to $1,000+ for national conventions. Finally, to understand what network marketing truly is, you'll be paying for books, lectures, and videos about the business and about personal growth—the heart of being successful.

So whatever the distributor says to the prospect about what it costs to build the business, his calculation is way too low.

As with any business, capital is needed to start it and then fund it as it grows. Many people drop out of network marketing because it costs too much to continue on the journey.

The Lie Corrected

I have been associated with companies where the initial investment was $5,000. I have seen others where the initial investment was $125. But by the time the options were explained, those prices had risen. More products would be needed to be in inventory to sell right away; the company offered extra services, such as advanced websites and training with additional costs. In most cases, there are extras that new distributors find hard to refuse because they think they will propel them to the top.

I am not saying those items are useless—far from it. In most cases, they are a must for a new distributor who is serious about building a business. But in the beginning, when the new people first heard about the opportunity, I bet they didn't envision the money that would be needed. The pressure to spend, from both the upline distributors and the company, is huge. The belief in NM that you have to continuously grow as a person and continuously read and learn is very demanding. Again, I'm not saying that all the tools and opportunities to grow aren't needed. But for most, they can come as a surprise.

What has to be said to avoid the lie? First, never say that all that is needed is a very small sum. Yes, the very first initial investment to register with the company may be small, but you should explain to the prospect what lies ahead monetarily. The distributor must ascertain what the prospect expects to earn and in what time frame. The distributor then has to tell the prospect what has to be done. Give the prospect a realistic idea of what the monthly costs may be, what will have to be spent on tools, and what additional money may be needed to travel to events. If this is not done, I can almost guarantee that over time, be it a couple of months or a year or two, the prospect will be gone from the business.

Lie 9.

"A start-up is the right company to join, because you will be the first one in and profit the most."

The Truth

This statement probably has the most appeal to someone who has been in NM before. They have seen other people succeed and believe that with a brand-new company, they can too. They probably don't understand that they might not overcome their lack of success in one company by starting over with a new one.

One of the first questions a prospect generally asks is, "How long has the company been in business?" Most people will want to hear that it is brand-new or just a year or two old. They believe that with a new company, they'll have a good chance to build their business. But the astute businessperson understands that many new businesses, particularly in network marketing, don't make it past one year.

As I mentioned previously, the two companies with which I was successful were not new companies. Yet I was able to reach the top ranks of both. Joining a start-up is not an advantage for a prospect who has had no previous success in NM. But for an experienced network marketer, there might be an advantage to going with one—a small advantage. The experienced distributor could bring many of her present downline with her. Her learning curve would be faster. And she could offer the opportunity to other network marketers with the enticement that it is a start-up. She could use this pitch to those who are not successful: "Come join my team in a start-up, and we will be one of the first teams in." But the only one who benefits in this scenario is the experienced networker. She will benefit from having others join under her. All the tools needed to be successful must still be obtained and learned.

The Lie Corrected

As I mentioned before, 90 percent of new companies entering the NM arena are gone within one to two years. New companies face a lot of challenges, among them proper financing: they are always chasing money. Product supply can become a huge problem too. The company might have a great product, but with demand growing fast, the product can become difficult to obtain or manufacture. Demand can cause huge supply problems. The unexpected usually turns up: poor product quality, supply-chain issues, consumer complaints, or a management that isn't aware of the unique aspects of the business model. These and other challenges are reason to stop and take a serious behind-the-scenes look at a start-up. Wait at least three years—most companies still in business by then will have had time to overcome these challenges.

So how should a distributor mention their company is a start-up to a prospect? A start-up is a company that's been in business less than two years—that's my definition. After that, it can be called a company that is just beginning its growth stage.

The fact that a company is a start-up should never be the lead reason for a prospect to join. If it is given as such, then you must also mention the caveats: "Jane, let me mention that this is a start-up. There are a couple of advantages to getting involved now and a couple of things you should be aware of." Then go ahead and explain both sides. Once she understands, you can always highlight the uniqueness of the product or the corporate leadership. As long as she knows the pros and cons, you can feel that you've done right by her.

Lie 10.

"No stress and a lot of time freedom."

The Truth

In any business that is your own business or in which you are the boss, there is going to be stress. Network marketing is no different. In fact, as your business grows, the stress will become even more intense. Let's examine the stress part of this statement first.

When a distributor makes this statement to a prospect, he is usually projecting what will be in the future as the new prospect builds his business. It is said to entice the prospect with the idea that the end result will be great. But if this ever happens, it will be far down the road, after a huge organization of other leaders has emerged on the team.

Here is the progression with stress: As you start your business, you are excited. The opportunity to build it and start assembling your team allows you to enjoy the new journey. Once this initial excitement wears off and the pressure of advancing in your company begins, the stress starts to emerge. First it comes from encountering rejection, which is not a happy experience and can wear on you. Then it comes from hearing from your upline what you have to do to advance in rank and help yourself and benefit your upline. It's not fun at all when you see that your actions affect others. The stress mounts.

Finally, you start to experience success. "Now," you say, "I am successful, so there won't be any stress." Wrong. Now you have a team under you who require your attention and help. Also, for you to continue to move upward, you'll need your downline team to work hard and be successful too. This is a new kind of stress: worrying about others and their success.

The amount of stress in network marketing is related to the success you desire and the team you build. It really never goes away. People will tell you that as your team gets bigger, your stress and worry about its growth will diminish. Not so. When I was making $40,000 per month, my worrying and stress did not diminish. First, you are always concerned about your downline and what you can do for them. Second, you are making good money but wonder, "What if it goes away?" You have heard that NM companies have failed and the checks have disappeared. Thus you can't stop building and supporting your team, because what if the unthinkable happened? This is a nonstop process.

When does the stress disappear? Only about half of 1 percent will ever reach the top echelon, where stress might disappear. That journey might take ten to fifteen years, and it is not guaranteed. So when you hear that there is no stress in network marketing, remember that it just isn't so.

It is much the same thing with time freedom. In building your network business, you actually *lose* time freedom. Once you start to understand the compensation plan and want to move up, time becomes extremely valuable, as you spend more and more time building. The larger your organization gets and the more you strive to reach the top, the less free time you will have. Like freedom from stress, time freedom never really appears until you reach the upper levels of the organization and have developed leaders under you to manage their business. Again, real time freedom occurs only at the top ranks and after a huge organization has been developed.

The Lie Corrected

When using the statement "no stress and time freedom," you have to clarify what those words mean. This claim can be corrected if it is used with an explanation and a caveat. Here is an example.

When speaking to prospect Bill, say, "Bill, one potential benefit of this business in the end is no stress and time freedom. Understand, though, that achieving these things will take a lot of work, long hours, and several years on your part. Actually, on your journey you *will* experience stress and little time freedom. But if you commit to working the business and learning the nuances of network marketing, there is a good possibility that you might be able to experience its true benefits down the line. Understand that it will take several years before it might come to fruition."

Lie 11.

"You will have successful people there
to help you."

The Truth

Theoretically, that is how the business model works.
Your upline should be there to help you grow your
business. It behooves them to do this, since they will
benefit from your success too. Then there is a team of
distributors above you—if they understand the compensation plan and their responsibilities, they should
be available to help you. The problem occurs when a
new distributor is abandoned by his sponsor, and no
one steps in to train the new member of the team. If
the new distributor is new to network marketing and
does not fully understand the business, he will floun-
der, get discouraged, and soon drop out.

Very few new distributors did what I did in my
first organization. My sponsor was in Florida and I
was in New Jersey. He would not come up and train
me, so I had to do it on my own. At least he sent me
videos to watch. The problem is harder the farther
you have to go to find someone to mentor and train

you. The deeper in the organization you go, the less incentive and time the upline has to help you. Time is in short supply if you are engaged in doing the business seriously. If the incentive is not there, the upline just cannot afford to work with you. Only rarely will you find someone deep in your organization or even crossline to help you. I was lucky in finding my mentor after two years in the business. He was a successful crossline. We bonded, and a real student-mentor relationship occurred. It can happen, but it is rare.

The Lie Corrected

Network marketing, truly understood, is a team business. No one can be successful alone. To succeed, you must help others succeed. It is that simple. When talking to a new prospect or distributor, you must make him aware that you will be there to train him. At the least, you will hook him into a system and a meeting where he can get the information needed to build a business. The sponsor must make the new distributor aware of his upline and introduce him, so he will know where to go when his sponsor cannot help. The sponsor must also make sure the new distributor knows how relationships and team building work. Some responsibility lies with the new distributor to reach out to the upline and ask if they will be available to help if needed.

Here something you can say to a new distributor or a prospect: "Bob [the distributor], network marketing is built on teamwork. One of my jobs is to make sure you are properly trained and introduced to the system and team. Understand it is your responsibility to learn the system and to reach out when you need help. I am your first choice, but you are not limited to me. Here is a list of your immediate upline. Check in with him and let him know you are serious about the business and hope he will help when needed."

This business is unique in that uplines make themselves more readily available to help the successful than those who are just starting out. I built my business on this statement, "Say no to the good and yes to the best." When confronted with a decision of where to go when two people ask for your help, I've always followed that statement. The best are committed, working, and producing. You do not ignore the good, but always respond to the best first.

Lie 12.

"Build it once and collect money while you relax on the beach."

The Truth

Having been in network marketing for over twenty-five years, I find it hard to believe this one. I guess it is possible to build it once and collect mailbox money while you relax on the beach, but in all my years in this field, I have not met anyone who falls in that category. Probably a few people have accomplished that, but not many. If they did, let's take a look at how they did it.

First, network marketing is built by promoting the dream. Find out why someone wants to succeed, and then promote the business opportunity on the chance that they will reach their dream. If that person does not see the path to success, they will jump ship and follow their dream with another company. This will continue to occur every time a roadblock appears and the dream does not seem accessible anymore. As a result, they never realize their full dream.

If a distributor begins to show positive results and can see his dream over the horizon, then he will work harder and harder as he gets closer. But here is the reality: as he earns more money and his lifestyle changes, he has to work as hard or harder to continue to chase his dream. Also, since his continued success is geared to the ability of his team and his company to continue to produce, he gets scared. He always has the thought, "What if something happens to the company, or my downline starts to abandon this company for another one? What will I do then?" So he works harder in order to ensure that income will grow. It is a catch-22. The more money he makes, the harder he works.

How do you build it once, then relax on the beach? It will take time. The best odds are staying with a well-run company for a long time—in the neighborhood of fifteen to twenty years. Develop a relationship with strong leaders in your downline. Never fully stop working with your leaders. Hopefully you will be able to take time off more often. But to be honest, it is a really rare situation where your income will remain stable while you sun yourself on the beach.

The Lie Corrected

Network marketing is a real business that must be constantly worked. When talking to prospects or new distributors, make sure they understand that this is a great part-time business that can be developed, over time, into a full-time business. But don't fall into the trap of teasing them with the idea that they can just build it in a few years and then relax on the beach from then on. Say something like this: "Bill, network marketing offers you the chance to develop a long-lasting business. It will take time but can be done with the right focus, persistence, and commitment. Like any business, it will have to be constantly managed, but in the end it can bring you true residual income."

Lie 13.

"Ultimate get-rich-quick opportunity."

The Truth

This saying is associated more than any other with network marketing, but getting rich quick is not what network marketing is about.

Again, let's analyze the statement. What is *rich*? *Rich* is different to each individual. To one person, rich can be $100,000. To another, it is $1,000,000, and to others it can be $10,000,000 and above. Each person is different, and their concept of a lot of money is personal.

What is *quick*? Again, a personal decision. Quick for one person can be a month. For another, it can be a year, and for others it can be three years or more. When one looks at the big picture and understands the dynamics of a business, quick is not a 100-yard dash—it is a marathon.

When we put both words together, "rich quick," they have a totally different meaning for each person. Yet in the hype of the moment, "get rich quick" excites people enough that they ignore the reality and what the words actually mean to them.

The Lie Corrected

This lie, more than any others, has given network marketing a bad reputation. People are enticed into the opportunity with the expectation that they will make a lot of money fast. For 99 percent of them, that will never happen. They will get discouraged and quit as they feel they aren't getting rich.

How do you correct that statement and give people the chance to truly experience the benefits of network marketing? When presenting the opportunity to prospects, be up-front and explain the business plan realistically.

In many presentations, you'll see a drawing that shows if you get two people to join and they get two people to join and on and on, within a year you'll have thousands of people in your organization, and you will be rich. In reality, this never happens. You might be able to get two people, but can they get two people, and can the next generation get two people? And if they could, is each person going to work hard and build a business? No.

Your responsibility is to be honest and explain the business plan and what has to be done to put the new distributor on the right track to success. You might say something like this: "Bob, our opportunity can afford you the chance to build an organization that can have the chance to generate income. How much income is going to be determined by the effort you put into growing your business. It won't happen overnight, but with persistent and consistent effort and with the help of our team, the real possibility is there for you to have a good income stream." Let the prospect know that work is required. The benefit is that the prospect won't get discouraged quickly. The thought of getting rich quick never enters his mind.

CHAPTER TWO

~

Discovering How to Build Your Business

Now that we understand why so many people get discouraged with network marketing, do not succeed, and leave with a negative attitude, let me lay the foundation for new distributors, distributors who are presently building their business, and successful distributors who want to help their teammates succeed.

When I started with this business model in 1994, there was only a limited supply of reading material available to educate new distributors. The Internet was several years away. We were in the age of the videotape, and the cell phone, at least as we know it today, had not been developed. Because of our more limited means of obtaining information, if a good communication system between a company and team members was not implemented, it was extremely hard for an individual to succeed.

In the years since, things have changed rapidly. Network marketing began to be accepted as a true business model. Books on the subject began to appear. Successful distributors started telling their stories. Entrepreneurs saw a need for how-to books for new network marketers. The videotapes were replaced by easier-to-use CDs, which contained more information at a more reasonable price. The Internet grew up, enabling teams to communicate and disseminate information faster. Finally, the cell phone became a device for all. It allowed distributors to run their businesses from anywhere in the world at any time of day.

Since I was alone in my business at the start, I searched for books to guide me on my journey. As more books started appearing, I made it my duty to read as many as time allowed. This indeed helped me better understand how the business worked. But after reading several shelves of books, I discovered that they basically all taught the same principles within their own personal stories. If a new book came out, I could predict what the author was going to describe. Each book had something unique to add, but the heart of what he wanted to leave the reader with was the same.

The first company I joined was a Japanese company that knew how important personal growth was to a distributor's success. If you had to ask me what, in all my years in the business, has had the biggest impact on my success, I'd say the programs initiated by that company. From that point on, I judged every company I got involved with and those I investigated by whether any could live up to what I'd been exposed to. None could. I was indeed lucky. Why? Because the heart of network marketing is a person's ability to grow as an individual in their relationships with themselves, with their friends, and with strangers they want to make part of their team.

Many excellent books on the market can give you the information you need about network marketing and personal growth. To make your learning easier, I've divided these books into three categories. The first includes books that strictly give you the steps you need to succeed. The beauty of this business is that there are not many steps, but the ones you learn must be learned well.

The second category entails the skills necessary to grow the business. These are more involved than the primary steps in the first category, though several of those books also touch on these skills. To reach the top in network marketing, these skills must be mastered.

The third category is books on personal growth. This subject is my favorite. I have far more books on this subject than on the basics of network marketing. When a new distributor joins my team, I always tell them that they will grow as a person on their journey in network marketing. This business is indeed transformational for everyone involved.

To build a successful network marketing business (and that is my wish for you), it is imperative that you absorb this information quickly. Of course, your company and upline will try to lock you into their system, and that is fine. But the basic information on network marketing is readily available, so don't wait for it to be delivered to you—go get it. Remember, your success is the responsibility of one person and one person alone: *you.*

Here is where you can obtain the foundation for your business. I have listed books by title, author, and date published. Some are older than others. But as I said, the basics of this business have not changed. What *has* changed is how the information is disseminated. In the network-marketing section, I have listed the books that have helped me grow my business and those that are legendary in the industry. All are worth the read. In the section on skills, I've listed books that deal solely with an individual skill. In the personal-growth section, I've listed those that had the biggest impact on me. Once you understand the importance of personal growth to your success, you can go on the Internet and find many other books on it—these are just my top choices. In two sections, I've included CDs that *must* be listened to.

Network Marketing Steps

These are the basic steps—the nuts and bolts—you must master in order to succeed:

1. Finding prospects
2. Inviting
3. Presenting
4. Follow-up
5. Sign-up procedure
6. Getting started
7. Promoting the event
8. Handling objections
9. Training and support
10. Duplication
11. Team building
12. Goal setting

The books below cover all the above steps. These are from my library. Are they the best and only ones written? *No.* They are the ones that helped me in my success. Many are older books, but as I said before, the information to be successful in NM has not changed. The key advice is to become a constant reader.

Network Marketing: Books

Being the Best You Can Be in MLM
by John Kalench (1990).

When I began my journey in NM, this book was my bible. It spelled out all the how-tos in a simple manner. I gave it to every person on my team and asked them to give it to their team. A true gem.

The Greatest Networker in the World
by John Milton Fogg (1997).

A little book that tells a story with a powerful message. To be read and reread in order to keep uncovering more and more valuable advice. As with the first book, I gave this as a gift to the members of my team. Every network marketer should read this.

Your First Year in Network Marketing
by Mark Yarnell (1998).

Hailed by NM veterans as a classic first read for learning the business.

Mach II with Your Hair on Fire
by Richard Brooke (2000).

More than a nuts-and-bolts book, this highlights the importance of vision and self-motivation in NM. A book that will be read and reread.

Go Pro: 7 Steps to Becoming a Network Marketing Professional by Eric Worre (2013).

As you can see from the date of publication, this is a relatively new book compared to the others on this list. *Go Pro* has become the book to read and be guided by for today's network marketers. It gives you a step-by-step action plan to become a network-marketing professional.

Dare to Dream and Work to Win: Understanding the Dollars and Sense of Network Marketing by Dr. Tom Barrett (1998).

An excellent book. The author delves into the foundation for success, the psychological side of success, and the power of leadership in network marketing. It's an easy read with a lot of great insight into what you need to be a success.

All You Can Do Is All You Can Do, But All You Can Do Is Enough by A. L. Williams (1988).

A motivational book by one of the true pioneers of the industry.

17 Secrets of the Master Prospectors by John Kalench (1994).

Wave 4 Network Marketing for the 21st Century by Richard Poe (1999).

The 45-Second Presentation That Will Change Your Life by Don Failla (2009).

Network Marketing: Action Guide for Success by David Stewart (1991).

Successful Network Marketing for the 21st Century by Rod Nichols (1995)

Network Marketing: Audio

Building Your Network Marketing Business by Jim Rohn (2000).

This is the best audio you will find on network marketing. Everyone in NM should listen to it over and over until all the information given is understood. If you are a leader, you should make sure every member of your team has this.

Skills: Books

Partnership Is the New Leadership by Ty Bennett (2016).

The Power of Influence by Ty Bennett (2017).

The Power of Storytelling by Ty Bennett (2018).

Years ago, I was on a retreat with one of my NM companies and met Ty Bennett, who was building a huge downline with his brother. After several years Ty sold his business to his brother and went to pursue his true passion, public speaking. He is now one of the most sought-after speakers in the country. He has written three books on subjects that are crucial to your success in NM: leadership, influence, and storytelling.

The 21 Irrefutable Laws of Leadership by John Maxwell (1998).

The 17 Indisputable Laws of Teamwork by John Maxwell (2001).

Simply put, John Maxwell is the number-one author and teacher on leadership. He has written countless books on leadership and teamwork. Any one of them could appear on this list. I chose these two because you can adapt what he talks about for NM. I have given speeches about both books. Add them to your library.

Leadership Is an Art by Max DePree (1989).

Listening for Success: How to Master the Most Important Skill of Network Marketing by Steve Shapiro (1999).

Every network marketer knows that the person in a conversation who is listening is the person who is winning. There is an art to listening, and Steve Shapiro explains it the best.

Personal Growth: Books

Think and Grow Rich by Napoleon Hill (1937).

I can assure you that all the successful network marketers have this book in their library and have read it several times. I make it a must-read once a year. The information in the book is extremely valuable for your success. If you read no other book, read this one.

How to Win Friends and Influence People by Dale Carnegie (1936).

Understand that you are in the people business and you need friends to win. Dale Carnegie is at the forefront of personal growth. Another must-read.

As a Man Thinketh by James Allen (1903).

A little book that is very impactful.

The Science of Getting Rich by Wallace D. Wattles (1910).

Another book written years ago that has stood the test of time.

Peak Performance Principles for High Achievers by John Noe (1984).

This book tells you what a high achiever looks like. If you are striving to get to the top, read it and see what you have to do to reach the summit.

The 7 Habits of Highly Effective People by Stephen Covey (1989).

A classic.

*Energy Leadership: Transforming Your
Workplace and Your Life from the Core*
by Bruce Schneider (2008).

Bruce Schneider shows you why the way
you use your energy determines whether your
organization thrives.

The Greatest Salesman in the World
by Og Mandino (1968).

The Greatest Miracle in the World
by Og Mandino (1975).

The Richest Man in Babylon
by George Clason (1926).

You Were Born Rich by Bob Proctor (1984).

Excellent book on personal growth. Helps
you recognize and make the changes necessary
to live your dreams.

*Working with the Law: 11 Truth Principles for
Successful Living* by Raymond Holliwell (1992).

*Rich Dad/Poor Dad: What the Rich Teach
Their Children That the Poor and Middle
Class Do Not!* by Robert Kiyosaki (1997).

Man's Search for Meaning by Viktor Frankl (1959).

If you think NM is challenging, read this book and put your life and journey into perspective.

Personal Growth: Audio

The Essence of Success by Earl Nightingale (1991).

This ten-CD set must be listened to and studied. You should be listening to it every time you are in your car. It is all about personal growth. I can assure you if you start to follow the information you hear about, life will take on a new and more powerful meaning.

Of course there are many other books, recordings, and videos that you can add to your library. Understand that this is not a sprint, it is a marathon, and as I've said, it can take five years to fully grasp how network marketing works. The final part of your success has to do with *you*.

CHAPTER THREE

~

Personal Growth: Energy Leadership

Network marketing, as I have said, is the best business model, because it creates a win/win situation for all involved. In chapter 1, I set the record straight so you could build a business based on truth and integrity. As you present the business to more and more people, allowing them to see how it grows, you will begin to feel more comfortable with your presentations. In chapter 2, I gave you the tools to build a solid foundation. Understanding the nuts and bolts of network marketing will take time, but as you become proficient in the skills needed to grow, your business will become more professional, and you will begin to attract people to you.

Once again, here are the skills that must be mastered:

1. Finding prospects
2. Inviting
3. Presenting
4. Follow-up
5. Sign-up procedure
6. Getting started
7. Promoting the event
8. Handling objections
9. Training and support
10. Duplication
11. Team building
12. Goal setting

Mastering these skills will enable you to build a team, develop leaders, duplicate your success, and finally obtain what is network marketing's true gift: leverage.

Personal growth is at the heart of success in NM. People who master the above steps might still not reach the top levels, because it is a people business. To be successful, you must first look at yourself and see where you are in understanding yourself and how you deal with others. As a life coach, I have worked with many people who feel they should be more successful. After working with them, I can quickly understand why they are not. Their attitude about themselves and the way they interact with others have kept them from succeeding. For most people, the hardest thing is to step outside of themselves and see how their attitude manifests itself with others. When I say it can take up to five years to understand NM, that is because it generally takes time for most people to start to understand themselves and begin to interact with other people with a full understanding of the situation.

There are three types of people in the world today: those who watch things happen, those who make things happen, and those who just say, "What happened?" As life goes by, people tend to fall into one of these three categories. Which one are you?

In NM many people tend to watch and go through the moves they think will bring them success. Others have no clue and simply ask after a while, "What just happened? Why am I not onstage?" Then there are those who make things happen. They develop teams; they understand what it takes to be a leader. Isn't that what we all strive for?

I believe we need to answer the question "Who is a leader?" A general definition could be "a person who influences people toward the achievement of a goal."

Many might say that a position of authority constitutes leadership. I disagree. A position of authority or rank is no guarantee. It does help in the sense that a leadership position usually commands a listening ear. But how many people in NM call themselves leaders because of their rank but have no influence over their downline? A true leader must have a deep-rooted commitment to the goal he strives to achieve, even if nobody follows him. With this commitment and goal must come a personal vision—the ability to visualize one's goal as an accomplished fact, a thing already achieved. The leader must realize that the goal cannot be achieved alone, without the help of others. The leader must be able to integrate his goals with his followers' goals so that they embrace it and the goal becomes a common goal.

Finally, one critical element of leadership is a love for people. You have to care about them. When people are convinced of your love for them and are sure that you always have their interests at heart, they trust you and will follow you unconditionally.

Energy Leadership

Energy Leadership refers to both a particular form of leadership and to the process of leading energy so that it works for you, not against you. It has two basic premises: (1) Everyone leads, either by choice or default. If you do not think of yourself as a leader, then your thinking is limited. Leading is the way we help move people into action, including ourselves. The question is not whether or not we are leaders, but how we lead. (2) The higher your overall energy level, the more successful and fulfilled you'll be. Studies show that this is true almost 100 percent of the time, whether it is measured in finances, fulfillment, peace of mind, relationships, or more: people who have the highest levels of consciousness have the most energy and report the most success in their lives.

Consciousness is the level of one's self-awareness, how one fully realizes his or her true self, as opposed to the self one has been trained to see and accept. Your true self is unlimited. Your level of consciousness is determined by how you see yourself, the world around you, the people in your life, and life in general. The higher your level of consciousness, the more energy you have, and the more productive, peaceful, powerful, and healthy you are. There is a direct relationship between consciousness and success.

Finally, it is important to understand what energy is and how it relates to you. Energy is one's potential for success in life. The best way to describe energy is to say it is our *potential output*. Our potential output is our overall energy, which is based on our level of consciousness or awareness about our potential. Our potential is unlimited, yet most people only tap into a fraction of it. We want to be able to tap into our full potential.

For our purposes here, there are two types of energy: *anabolic energy*, which is constructive, and *catabolic energy*, which is destructive. When the mind perceives a threat, anabolic hormones, such as testosterone, decrease, while catabolic hormones, such as cortisol and adrenalin, increase. The increase in catabolic hormones serves a short-term purpose by creating enough physical energy to meet the stressor. However, on a long-term basis, a constant release of catabolic hormones causes the entire bodily system to deteriorate.

Both types of hormonal releases stem from thoughts, and so thoughts are either anabolic or catabolic. Each of us has trained ourselves to automatically react to many of our life situations. These "default tendencies," if catabolic, actually cannibalize our entire system.

Anabolic leaders have the ability to motivate and inspire themselves and others to do extraordinary things. They have the ability to make energetic shifts in all levels of their team. Catabolic leaders break down all aspects of the team.

Your level of energy, being either catabolic or anabolic, will determine your success. Catabolic energy is the energy of worry, frustration, and blame. If not *checked, this can lead to a toxic environment. Anabolic energy is constructive and fuels creativity. Someone with anabolic energy can motivate and inspire others to do extraordinary things and can promote positive outcomes and incredible change within every area of life. Your thoughts determine your feelings, and your feelings dictate your actions. Thus what a person thinks and feels about themselves and the people they associate with will create their world.**

Your "resonant frequency" is your natural frequency. When you align with it, your work and life become effortless. It could be said that your natural frequency is something you rarely use, or would definitely like to use more, as it's the highest frequency available to us.

We are naturally all highly conscious at our core—it's our "humanness" that gets in the way. A part of our brain is always scanning our surroundings for things that are problematic, familiar, or out of place and always tries to make sense of what we see in a way we can understand. The challenge is that our default tendencies get us to notice and perceive

---

* The italicized thoughts in this chapter have come from my participation in the iPEC coaching program and the Energy Leadership Development System. The original thoughts on Energy Leadership, consciousness, and levels of energy all originate from Bruce Schneider and iPEC Coaching. Many of the descriptions and thoughts I explain below have been taken from iPEC's Energy Leadership Development System Workbook.

the same things in the same way over and over again. So now our brain picks up a thing as familiar and possibly problematic. It continues to point out these common situations, concerns, and frustrations over and over again. Unless you interrupt this pattern, you will see the same things repeatedly: you will never see things differently.

Energy Leadership is a way of interrupting this process of the brain so that you can consciously decide what you want to see in your surroundings and in others and yourself. This change enables you to place things you want to notice in your brain so that you can break this self-perpetuating cycle. It will develop an effective style of leadership that positively influences and changes not only you, but also those with whom you work and interact, as well as your team as a whole.

When I speak of energy, I'm not referring only to physical energy. I'm also referring to emotional, mental, psychological, and even spiritual energy. Mostly I'm referring to your particular energetic profile. We are energetic beings, and based on how we think, feel, and act, we are constantly experiencing and sharing either anabolic energy, which works for us, or catabolic energy, which works against us.

There are actually seven levels of energy, or consciousness, at which we can resonate. Our Average

Resonating Level of energy (ARL) falls somewhere on this scale, between one and seven; it comprises the sum total of every thought we've ever had, every emotion we've ever felt, and every action we've ever taken, as well as those we are thinking, feeling, and doing at present. Your ARL is the average of all your day-to-day thoughts.

Each person's energy level varies based on certain life aspects, including their job. No two people have the same energetic makeup. Like a stock, your energy level can go up or down, depending upon how you perceive and respond to what's happening in your life. Your ARL determines your energetic makeup, view of the world, physical and mental health, ability to lead, and level of success.

People resonating at lower levels tend to attract negative things and react in kind—a black cloud follows them around—while those resonating at higher levels attract and experience more ease, opportunity, power, and success. They seem to have the Midas touch. Here is the great news: we have the ability to alter our energy level, our level of consciousness— and that has a huge impact on our daily actions, the people on our team, those we live with, and our own bodies. In fact, your energy level—your ARL—is the number-one factor determining your level of success in life.

As we have discussed, success in NM is not about your ability to sell. It is about your ability to become a leader and to find and develop leaders. The key components of NM are *duplication* and *leverage*. To obtain them, you must become a leader. Your ability to lead effectively relates to your level of energy. Your current state of consciousness is composed of your existing energetic makeup, which encompasses every thought, feeling, and emotion you've had today, as well as your recent actions.

In Bruce Schneider's Energetic Self-Perception Chart, there are seven levels of Energy Leadership. The chart allows you to see where you are by looking at your attitude and your perception of and perspective on your world. Because attitude is subjective, it can be altered. By working on your attitude and perspective, you can shift your consciousness and increase your energy. Once you understand and see your potential, there are no limits to the growth you can achieve.

In the first chapter of this book, I emphasized the importance of starting and building your business with honesty and integrity. One can ask for no better foundation than that. In the second chapter, I directed you to the information that can educate you to allow you to grow your business. In this final chapter, I offer you the insight and awareness you need to develop into a true leader and recognize those who want to duplicate your leadership qualities. You'll find the Energetic Self-Perception Chart below. Let's go through the seven levels and explore how you can utilize this in your NM business and life.

Energetic Self Perception

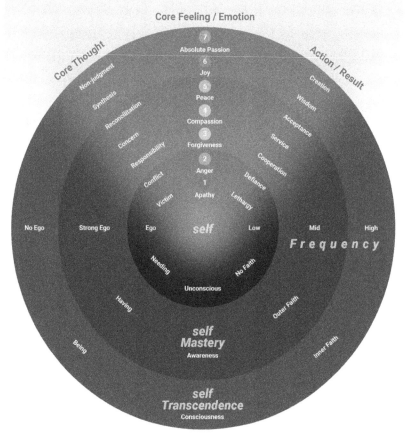

© Bruce D. Schneider 1999, 2006, 2018

As we go through the levels, try to recognize which negatively or positively influence aspects of your life, concentrating on how those levels relate to your leadership ability. Once you can identify the level you are on, you can make the attitude adjustments and thoughts necessary to progress to the next level. Understand that you can vary from one level to the next depending on circumstances. Once you're able to see how you expend your energy, you will be able to focus on the area that is most productive and allows you to deal with your team on a higher level. Being honest with yourself is of utmost importance to help your growth and ability to deal with people in the NM arena and in life.

Each level is exponentially more powerful than the one beneath it. I'm not saying the higher levels are "better," only higher. What you do with this information is your choice—and each level of energy has both its advantages and disadvantages.

Level 1

Role: The Victim
Main Thought: I lose.
Core Thought: Victim
Core Feeling/Emotion: Apathy
Action/Result: Lethargy

Catabolic energy is found on Level 1 and is displayed in the following thoughts and actions: I hate myself (low self-esteem); don't try, it will only lead to failure and rejection (self-doubt); no one listens or cares about me (indifference); I am not capable (guilt); failure follows me everywhere I go (victim); why bother, nothing changes (apathy).

Characteristics of the network marketer at level 1:

1. They are working in a crisis mode. They are always trying to qualify and look for new prospects at the last moment.

2. They are drawn to problems, and thus fail to see where progress lies. Focusing on the problems,

they fail to see the solution. They only look at the situations that take most of their time; they are not working with the people who can move them forward in their business.

3. They are scared to prospect and try new ways to build their business, because they are afraid they will fail.

4. Because of their poor self-image, they are constantly blaming themselves for not doing better and for negative things that happen. They feel they are not qualified to reach the top ranks.

5. At this level, they don't engage in tasks that will help them grow their business (such as going to events).

6. They have no ability to lead others, so they will never be able to build a team. If they have a downline, these individuals will get discouraged and will in all probability disappear.

7. Since they have a victim mentality, they believe they have the wrong sponsor, joined too late to succeed, and are on the wrong team.

8. Finally, they believe they can't succeed and consider themselves a loser.

If you see yourself in level 1, you must make changes to succeed in NM. Take a deeper look at yourself and see where you have to change. Look for books in the personal-growth section in chapter 2 and for others that you can research. If you are really serious about progressing in NM, seek out a life coach who can work with you and help you better understand and move you forward to change. (More on life coaching at the end of this chapter).

Level 2

Role: The Fighter

Main Thought: I win, you lose.

Core Thought: Conflict

Core Feeling/Emotion: Anger

Action/Result: Defiance

Catabolic energy is still present at this level and is exhibited in the following thoughts and actions: places their needs before those of others; goal is to come out ahead; one fight after another; they can win as long as someone else loses; it's a dog-eat-dog world; people only listen to me if they benefit from me; my worth is based on what I have achieved; I must control all aspects of my life; it's your fault.

Characteristics of the network marketer at level 2:

1. Goal is to win at all costs. In building the business, the individual will place themselves ahead of the team, with the sole purpose of achieving their rank with no consideration for others on their team.

2. Believe they can do anything better than others, thus fail to properly delegate, to the detriment of the team.

3. Always judging people and not giving them a chance to grow, thus making them feel they are not good enough.

4. Do not give recognition to others, which is a key ingredient for success in network marketing.

5. They tend to micromanage. They do not think of the big picture of where the team needs to go, only thinking of the present and how it affects them.

6. They motivate by aggression, fear, and force, which in some instances can lead to success, but is not duplicable and does not lead to a healthy team atmosphere.

7. Because of their behavior, they will not inspire others, and eventually this will lead team members to give up and quit.

Network marketers who are at this level will tend to succeed at first. They will make headway because of their philosophy of "win at any cost." With their aggressive style, they will move quickly in prospecting and growing their team. But as the team grows, they will leave people behind, partly because of their treatment of team members, but mostly because their "I win, you lose" philosophy will begin to be noticed. With little recognition given and no sincere inspiration, the downline will gradually feel neglected and lose the desire to continue with the opportunity.

Level 3

Role: The Rationalizer

Main Thought: I win; if you win too, great.

Core Thought: Responsibility

Core Feeling/Emotion: Forgiveness

Action/Result: Cooperation

Anabolic energy starts to become present here. Because of that, other beneficial core thoughts start to appear: I forgive you; life is what you make of it; you can create a purpose and live guided by it, with the right connections; I will overcome each hurdle; have a good plan, but will do it only if sure it will work; what I can't see can't hurt me; I am in control of my life, and I know how to "play the game"; I am sure I can convince them to see it my way (persuades); my view of life and those in it are completely up to me; people are generally good, they just don't know better; the past is not important, let's live for today (said, but not believed); I can do better; better to lie and avoid than to face conflict.

The members on your team with level 3 energy resonate with the beginnings of anabolic energy. They generally are positive and productive, dealing with solu-

tions instead of problems. The key component to success is attitude. With a positive attitude, level 3 members handle situations much differently than level 1 and 2 members, who have catabolic energy. Instead of reacting to emotions, they know how to work with emotions to manage them within themselves and in others. When a crisis or challenge arises, they'll move to resolve it confidently and tactfully, responding with logic instead of reacting with emotion.

Some of the advantages of members with this level of energy: They don't allow other people to stand in the way of what they want; the ability to avoid, block, and/or release negativity of others; able to engage others with promises and hopes. Though these level 3 members have made the turn to becoming productive, they still have some challenges to overcome: They can be manipulative and self-concerned; their hopes and promises are not always given from the heart, but the head; they can be unconcerned about whether things work out because they "did their best."

Characteristics of the network marketer at level 3:

1. At this level, your distributor is interested in taking responsibility to get things done. They

are not fully committed to the team yet, as it is still about them winning.

2. They have a plan, but to succeed they play the "persuade" game. They don't listen to their prospects and team members' voices; they try and persuade them to do it their way.

3. These distributors are concerned with today and how it will affect him. They are unable to paint a vision of where the team and the company will be in the future.

4. They believe they can be successful and will try, but if they are not successful, they can live with it, because they believe they did their best. The key ingredient of the successful network marketer is the belief "I will do whatever it takes." The Level 3 distributor is not there yet.

5. In network marketing, the distributor has to be able to listen to and deal with his team members. Dealing with emotions both within himself and in others is a challenge. The level 3 distributor is better able to react and deal with the emotions in a positive way.

6. Level 3 distributors are better able to handle the response "no" than level 1 and 2 distributors. They are able to move on and continue the process of prospecting and building.

7. In network marketing, crises inevitably appear every so often, such as product shortages, weather challenges during big events, or a top leader leaving. The level 3 distributor will deal with these situations using logic instead of getting emotional. They respond not with panic, which can really discourage their downline, but in a thoughtful manner.

In summary, a level 3 distributor has made the attitude change from having catabolic energy to using anabolic energy for his benefit. Even though their main objective is "me first," they are prepared to start to develop a team and build their business with a positive attitude. Though not fully committed to the total team concept that is needed in network marketing, they have the potential to be successful. Whether they continue on the path to develop the growth that is necessary to get to the next level remains to be seen.

Once you can identify a team member with this attitude, start to work with him and guide him. It is much easier to get a level 3 to the next level than to get a Level 1 or 2 to move up the energetic scale. Remember, in NM it is about developing leaders. The faster you can identify future leaders, the more promising the opportunity for you and your team.

Level 4

Role: The Caregiver
Main Thought: You win.
Core Thought: Concern
Core Feeling/Emotion: Compassion
Action/Result: Service

Anabolic energy is present at this level. Other core thoughts at this level are: I love you; how can I help you?; nothing feels better than service to others; our purpose is to give and help; your purpose is to make the world a better place; we can work this out; there's no need to control anything, but I like it when I feel life works; there is always something I can do to be a better person; the past does not matter, let's live and love now; I always strive to do better for everyone involved in my life.

People with level 4 energy are able to form deep relationships with others. People they work with respect them and see them as trustworthy. They are extremely loyal and willing to stand up for them as if for family. Whereas level 3 leaders mostly incorporate logical analysis to make decisions, level 4 leaders include emotional intelligence. They are concerned not only about their business but about the people they work with.

Characteristics of the network marketer at level 4:

1. At this level, the network marketer has become a team leader. It is no longer about himself but about the team.

2. They will constantly ask how they can help you: "When can we do three-way calls?" "When would you like me to conduct a meeting at your home for you?" "Can I help you with anything?"

3. They are always working for the team. They set up the weekly meetings; they help organize regional and national events. They make sure everyone can get to the events.

4. They are able to delegate, since that is the way their downline grows.

5. They will work for you constantly. If you cannot go to a meeting to meet prospects, they will go in your place.

6. They understand the power of recognition and are constantly recognizing team members.

7. They want to make sure everyone is aware of what is happening in the company and with the team. To do that, they set up a communication system to keep everyone up to date. This can be done with newsletters, emails, conference calls, Zoom calls, and other communication tools.

8. They are constantly training downlines at training meetings or face-to-face.

9. They go on the road to help those distributors not in their area. This might entail traveling several hours by car or taking a plane to a location either in the United States or in another country. They understand loyalty.

10. One drawback of the level 4 leader is that they are motivated more by being liked than by being productive. This might lead to poor time management at times and might hurt their own business.

11. The Level 4 leader will work with crossline, since the goal is the success of all.

12. They understand the power of listening. In network marketing, there is a saying: "Nobody cares

how much you know until they know how much you care." In order to show people you care, you must know how to listen.

The level 4 distributor is serious about the business and exhibits leadership qualities. They are building a downline and are working to duplicate themselves in order to develop downline leaders. Your goal is to develop and lead as many level 4 distributors as you can. They truly build the foundation of the business.

Level 5

Role: The Opportunist
Main Thought: We both win.
Core Thought: Reconciliation
Core Feeling/Emotion: Peace
Action/Result: Acceptance

Core thoughts present at this level: I want to understand you; life offers us opportunity after opportunity, you only have to open your eyes to see them; each person has a unique gift and the ability to use the gift to be successful; everything in life has meaning and purpose, and I want to know what it all means; success comes from within, and it is always up to me to feel successful; our purpose is to find peace and joy; our objective in life is to live it to the fullest and make a difference to as many people as possible—your value is in the way you do that; I only win if you win; I am always in control of my life and my perspective of it; everything always works out for the best, even if you don't see it that way at the time; I continually get better and better; I don't do the past.

The leaders with level 5 energy are powerful, inspiring, and skilled at capitalizing on whatever opportunities present themselves. At such high levels of resonance, by their presence alone, these leaders command greatness from others. They also expect greatness from others and receive it. Level 5 leaders see their team as gifted and full of potential. Level 5 leaders look for opportunities in partnerships and alliances, always thinking of synergy. Leaders at this level operate with less fear than do people at the levels below, and so have the willingness to enact radical change when warranted. Level 5 leaders find opportunities in all challenges; take little to nothing personally.

Characteristics of the network marketer at level 5:

1. Level 5 leaders are found at the top ranks in their companies. They are the leaders we see onstage speaking at the conventions.

2. They are the motivators onstage or one-on-one with their team.

3. At this level, they live their lives with a true sense of peace. Thus prospecting becomes very easy. They believe they can make a difference in everyone's life.

4. They are always looking for ways to build their team. They will think outside the box if it means helping their team grow.

5. Their main goal for the team is, "I only win if you win. Let's see what can be done to help you build your team. Let's strategize and make it happen."

6. Nothing will stop them in their drive for the win/win situation. If a challenge arises, they change it into an opportunity. When challenges appear, such as product disruption, management changes, and field leadership objections, the level 5 leader finds a silver lining and continues moving forward.

7. The level 5 leader never stops demanding greatness from their downline and receives it. Constant accountability from the downline is always present. They expect positive results and the downline is motivated to achieve them.

The level 5 distributor has made the jump to becoming a true leader in the organization. They have taken over their organization, and their downline now sees them as the team's leader. If you can develop three to five members of your team into level 5 leaders, you will truly be on your way to your dreams.

Level 6

Role: The Visionary
Main Thought: Everyone always wins.
Core Thought: Synthesis
Core Feeling/Emotion: Joy
Action/Result: Wisdom

Core thoughts present at this level: life itself is a wonderful opportunity; the purpose of life is to live and experience; I don't look at things as good or bad, they just are; "I" is the same as "we"; success is remembering who we really are; I'm open to life's mysteries, nothing needs to be figured out; everything I do, everyone does; there is no need to try to control life; there is power in partnerships—together, we can create miracles; the game of life cannot be won or lost, only played; everything is always working out as it happens; I continue to learn more about who we are and what life is about without trying.

Leaders at this level are highly active and willing to do anything they'd ask anyone else to do; these individuals lead by presence more than by actions. They are role models others look up to as wise, kind, and fair.

These leaders seem to know all that is going on in their teams without having to ask. They have a keen sense of intuition and use it on a regular basis to make decisions and to generate ideas.

Level 6 leaders are powerful, yet humble. They know their level of excellence and are still interested in growing. They listen to feedback from others about how they're leading and being perceived, and take action, without any ego blocks, to improve.

Such leaders share in projects instead of fully delegating them. By participating, the leader demonstrates a real connection to the team. The main characteristic that separates level 6 leaders from others is their ability to see all team members as equal to each other and to themselves. Level 6 leaders recognize that everyone is gifted. Because this is so, they help others realize their true potential, generating in this process a team of genuine and deeply committed partners, instead of people who are just workers. This is not to suggest that level 6 leaders believe in equal compensation or authority. They understand the nature of supply and demand and realize that people's specific talents should be compensated accordingly. Yet they also grasp a vital realization: without their team to support them, these leaders themselves would achieve little success.

Characteristics of the network marketer at level 6:

1. At level 6, the network marketer would be at the top level in their company. They are considered the rock stars of the organization.

2. The level 6 distributor is the true innovator. They will find ways to grow the business when others get frustrated.

3. The level 6 leader can be counted on to do anything they ask their downline to do. If they promote a team event, they will be there. If the company is holding a national convention, the level 6 leader will notify the team but will be the first one to commit to attending.

4. They are constantly aware of how their downline is doing. They make a point of seeing who is growing their teams, who is leading their teams in the right direction, who are the upcoming leaders who are committed to move up in the organization. They do this by just observing and listening to their downline.

5. The level 6 leader knows their position and realizes that they are looked up to, yet they are still looking to become better leaders. You will find them recommending new books to read, seminars to attend, and personal-growth events. Of course, they themselves have read these books and attended these events.

6. They have no ego and are quick to accept feedback from their downline. They will make known that if something can be done better, such as trainings, previews, or conference calls, they will welcome the feedback.

7. When it comes time to put on special events, the level 6 leader is right beside his team, demonstrating he is one of them and not above them.

8. For the level 6 distributor, it is all about the journey, not the rank or the money. It is not about winning or losing, only playing the game. The level 6 distributor truly enjoys the process of just building the business.

9. Level 6 leaders see the good in the whole team. No one is better than another. They inspire the team members to reach their true potential.

10. They do not judge any team member and connect with all. This allows the level 6 leader to bring the team together as one with the benefit for all.

The level 6 distributor has reached the top ranks of the company and has maximized the compensation plan. In most instances, they probably have surpassed you in rank, and that is a good thing. Your sole job in NM is to help your downline reach the top. Remember, if you have built your organization correctly, you will truly benefit from level 6 distributors in your organization.

Level 7

Role: The Creator
Main Thought: Winning and losing are illusions.
Core Thought: Nonjudgment
Core Feeling/Emotion: Absolute Passion
Action/Result: Creation

There are no examples of leaders that have an average resonating energy level at Level 7. They don't exist. In this state, no words are spoken, no picture can be created, and no examples can be provided. At level 7, the three-dimensional world that we think we know and see fades into pure energy.

Those who learn how to resonate at this level, even for a few moments, have access to Truth, and, in turn, can engage their natural genius to consciously create their world. At level 5, people try to find the silver lining from challenging experiences. At level 6, they see opportunities in all experiences. At level 7, people's creative ability is constant. At this level, we can use any of the below levels as we choose, create anything we desire, and do that as quickly as we believe. At level 7, we are connected to an intelligence of the highest order. We create our world as we choose.

At level 7, there is no right or wrong, good or bad, better or worse. Unconditional love is our true nature.

Incorporating this Knowledge

Having seen how important your energy level can be to your success, you must understand how to take this information and incorporate it into building your business. First, see where you fit into the Energetic Chart. To do that, look inside yourself and ascertain your attitudes, feelings, and actions. This is not easy, and in most instances cannot be done alone. One can read books and go to seminars to try to understand what can propel them to a more successful life.

As I have mentioned previously, another way to help you navigate the challenges that you might have is by working with a life coach. A life coach is not there to delve into your history, but to help you move forward in a more positive way. By working closely with you, helping you find the answers to the challenges in your life, the life coach can be the missing ingredient in your success.

I have found that the best way to see exactly how you place on the Energetic Self-Perception Chart is to take the Energy Leadership Index Assessment. Developed by Bruce Schneider, PhD, MCC, founder of iPEC Coaching, after twenty-five years of research into human potential and consciousness, this assessment provides insights into how you show up in your life as a leader. It measures your potential leadership awareness about who you are and what life is about.

Studies prove that higher levels of consciousness are associated with higher levels of success, including success in finances, relationships, personal development, and achievement. The assessment measures your ability to lead people, including yourself, to take positive, productive, and sustainable action. It also measures how involved or engaged you are in your roles and tasks on the job and at home. In summary, the energetic profile measures your *leadership ability*—your ability to inspire yourself and others to get more done; your *current level of engagement in life* (are you emotionally and intellectually involved, or simply going through the motions?); and your *current level of consciousness*—your awareness of who you truly are and what life is about.

Over the years I have coached several struggling network marketers. Working with them, I was able to help them see where they were stuck in their ability to grow their business. Were they able to go on to change and become successful with their business? Some were able to take the steps needed to move ahead. Others were not able to overcome their own personal challenges. Yet as a life coach, I was able to help them discover where each needed to change in order to grow.

As I have said earlier, networking marketing is not for everyone, and thus the help of a life coach will not succeed with someone not willing to change. But for those who are committed to personal growth, the life coach can be that guide to success.

A final word on life coaches: There are many people who claim to be life coaches. There are several companies that people can work with to become life coaches. If you look for a life coach, make sure they have come from a reputable company. If they specialize in business or better yet, network marketing, that would be great. I graduated from iPEC, one of the top coaching programs. I work with only a few people at a time, as my time is limited. I only take clients in the network marketing industry, as that is where I can consider myself a true student.

All my clients take the Energy Leadership Index Assessment. From those results, I work with a client to target the areas where they need improvement and understanding. The length of time I work with someone can vary from three months to a year or more.

The success of life coaches is well documented. If you are at a crossroads with your business now, but are serious in continuing your journey, take a serious look at working with a life coach. If you would like to talk to me about coaching and taking the Energy Leadership Index Assessment, please feel free to do so. I truly believe that every person in the network marketing industry should take this assessment to see where their energy level is. My contact information is at the end of the book.

CHAPTER FOUR

∼

What Next?

Network marketing is a genuine opportunity for those who are truly prepared to build a business. When I was with my first company, I always sat down with a prospect and asked questions to see what they wanted from the opportunity and how serious they were. To get a feel for the direction they wanted to go in, I always asked them what they were prepared to do to be successful. When I heard the magic words, *I will do whatever it takes,* I knew I had a serious prospect. I had a game plan in place for those serious prospects, and if they stuck to it, I was prepared to be with them every step of the way.

Network marketing is not a difficult business, but it does take a real commitment of time and educating oneself to be successful. The level of success one wants to achieve is directly proportionate to the commitment of time one wants to allocate to all aspects of the business. Understanding that network marketing, at its heart, is about finding and building leaders, you have to be committed to understand how to prospect and train and lead others so they can duplicate your efforts and go on to build their team.

In this book, I have given you a road map to begin your journey or to help you improve your present situation. The beauty of network marketing is that you can always reignite your business.

Build your business with integrity and truth. Don't promote it with false assumptions and false hopes. Become an avid reader, and build up a true library in all aspects of the business; learning the tools, learning the skills, and learning about personal growth.

Finally, I always tell people that if they are serious in building their business, they will change as individuals. Learning about yourself and why you do certain things is truly eye-opening. It is extremely rewarding in dealing with people you love, your friends, and your new business associates.

My journey in network marketing has been life-changing. In addition to the money (which has been nice), the chance to travel the world, the friendships I've made, and the people I've affected positively have been truly special. The opportunity for you is there; it is up to you to seize it and do *whatever it takes.*

For those who'd like to talk about taking the Energy Leadership Index Assessment or about coaching with one of the coaches on my team or myself, please feel free to reach out to me.

Phil Benson
philbenson@optimum.net
www.experiencelifecoaching.com

If you are interested in taking the Energy Leadership Index Assessment, go to my website and follow the procedure to sign up.

ABOUT THE AUTHOR

Phil Benson followed in his dad's footsteps, becoming an entrepreneur right away by starting several businesses. Having built a successful insurance agency, Phil quickly saw the power of residual income. When introduced to network marketing, he grasped the component of leverage, which makes the residual income even more powerful.

Understanding that the world was his marketplace, Phil built an international business in fifteen countries, with thousands of distributors in his organization over the next twenty-five years. Realizing his natural ability to work with individuals on a personal basis, Phil got his certification in Life Empowerment

Coaching and Core Energy Coaching from iPEC, one of the leading companies in the life-coaching industry. Phil has begun helping people reach their full potential by utilizing the vehicle of Energy Leadership coaching.

With this book, Phil has combined his expertise in both fields, network marketing and Energy Leadership coaching, to create a powerful guide that can be used to help all on their journey to success.